Previous page: Picasso's Night Fishing at Antibes, *1939.*
Below: A view of Montmartre, Paris. The white church on the hill is the Sacre-Coeur.

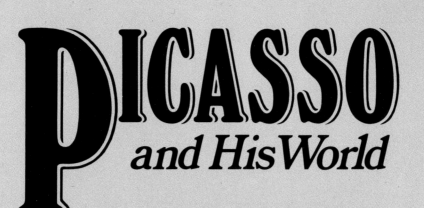

PICASSO
and His World

Terry Measham

SILVER BURDETT

Contents

Editorial

Author
Terry Measham

Editor
Christopher Fagg

Illustrator
Owain Bell

For Ant, Tom and Phil

Above left: Picasso's painting of his studio at Villa La Californie, Cannes, in 1955.
Left: Picasso at 74.

RT

A KINGFISHER BOOK

Published in the United States by
Silver Burdett Company, Morristown, New Jersey.

1980 Printing

ISBN 0-382-06376-7
80-68209
Designed and produced by Grisewood & Dempsey Limited,
Grosvenor House, 141-143 Drury Lane, London WC2.
© Grisewood & Dempsey Limited 1980
All rights reserved.
Printed and bound in Italy

The Modern Age

In 1900, the year when Pablo Picasso made his first visit to Paris, Sigmund Freud published his influential *The Interpretation of Dreams* in Vienna. In this and other works, Freud suggested that dreams, jokes, accidents and childhood experiences were all closely linked with the way that human beings live in and understand the world. At the same time, artists and writers were beginning to realize afresh the strange and intricate workings of the human mind. In science, the theories of Albert Einstein, first published in 1904, overturned all existing ideas of space, time, matter and energy. Already, in the 19th century, Charles Darwin's Theory of Evolution had undermined the ancient idea that Man was a special creation, set apart from the animals. So the 20th century, *our* century, opened with doubts and questionings. In art, too, great changes took place. For five centuries paintings had imitated surface appearances. But now artists turned away from European traditions and looked for inspiration to the cultures of so-called "primitive" societies. Led by painters like Picasso, Braque, Modigliani and Mondrian, Modern Art developed new techniques to express the Modern Age – an age of swift progress and disturbing uncertainties.

Picasso's Woman with Baby Carriage, *1950. From 1914 on, Picasso revolutionized sculpture by his use of everyday objects, discarded junk and so on. Here an odd collection of bits and pieces have been welded together to make a strong and recognizable image – then unified by being cast in bronze.*

7

Picasso's World

Picasso spent more than three-quarters of his life in voluntary exile in France. But he always remained, in the deepest sense, a Spaniard. He never forgot his birthplace, Málaga, which he often revisited. Madrid too, was a vital source of inspiration: there he had first studied the masterpieces of El Greco, Velasquez and Goya which greatly influenced his work. But, in his youth, Spain was cut off from the latest developments in art. It was necessary to travel to one of the great European centers of artistic and intellectual activity – cities like Vienna, Berlin, Munich, Brussels, Glasgow, London and, above all, Paris. In the Paris of 1900, thronged with visitors to the International exhibition, Picasso found the vitality and freedom needed for the exchange of new ideas and attitudes. He remained based there until the end of World War II. After that war, Picasso moved to the South of France. It was the closest he could get to his Mediterranean origins in Spain, which for political reasons he refused to visit. In Provence or Antibes, Picasso felt close to the birthplace of European civilization.

PAINTERS WORKING IN FRANCE:

Braque 1882–1963
(Artist)

Cézanne 1839–1906
(Artist)

Derain 1880–1954
(Artist)

Duchamp 1887–1968
(Artist)

Léger 1881–1955
(Artist)

Matisse 1869–1964
(Artist)

Monet 1840–1926
(Artist)

Pissarro 1834–1918
(Artist)

Toulouse-Lautrec
1864–1901 (Artist)

Vlaminck 1876–1958
(Artist)

SCOTLAND

Glasgow •

Joyce 1882–1941   **Moore** b. 1898
(Writer)   (Sculptor)

DH Lawrence 1885–1930
(Writer)

Sheffield 1950

ENGLAND

Mann 1875–1955
(Writer)

Mondrian 1872–1944   TO HOLLAND 1905
(Artist)   • Amsterdam

Elgar 1857–1934 • London 1919/1950   **Van Gogh** 1853–1890
(Composer)   (Artist)   • Berlin

Beardsley 1872–1898 • Brussels   TO POLAN
(Artist)   1948

Magritte 1898–1967   **Ernst** b.1891
(Artist)   (Artist)   GERMANY   **Kafka** 1883–
                                                     1924 (Writer)

Le Tremblay • La Rue-des-Bois 1908   **Einstein** 1879–1955
                                         (Physicist)

Dinard 1922/1928/1929 • 1936/1939 •   • Paris First visit 1900   **R Strauss** 1864–1949
                                                                    (Composer)   **Freud** 1856–1939
Boisgeloup 1930   **Proust** 1871–1922   (Psychoanalyst)
                                       (Writer)

                          Fontainebleau 1921   **Hesse** 1877–1962   **Hitler** 1889–1945
                                                 (Writer)   Munich •   (Dictator)   • Vienn
Breton 1896–1966
(Writer)   **Klee** 1879–1940 • Zurich   AUSTRIA
            FRANCE   (Artist)   **Schoenber**
          • Royan 1939/1940   SWITZERLAND   1874–1951
                                                          (Composer)

Le Corbusier 1887–1965   • Milan   **Pirandello** 1867–1936
(Architect)   (Dramatist)

• Corunna 1891–95   Sorgues 1912   TO ITALY 1917/1957

Franco 1892–1976   Avignon 1914 •   Saint-Raphael 1919   **Modigliani** 1884–192
(Dictator)   Biarritz 1918   Vauvenargues 1959 •   Monte Carlo 1925   (Artist)

Perpignan 1954   Cannes 1927/1933/1934/1955–61
Céret 1911/1912/1913 • • Collioure 1954   Juan-les-Pins 1920/1924/1925
Horta de San Juan 1898/1909 • Gosol 1906 •   • Cadaqués 1910   1926/1930/1931/1936   **Apollinaire** 1880–
            • Madrid   Cap d'Antibes 1923   1918 (Poet)
            1897/1901/1917/1934   Barcelona 1895–1900   Mougins 1936/1937/1938/1961–73
SPAIN   Toledo 1934   1901/1902/1903/1904   Antibes 1939   ITALY
                                   1917/1918/1933/1934   Golfe Juan 1945/1946/1947
            Dali b.1904   Vallauris 1948/1955
            (Artist)

Bunuel b.1900
(Film Director)

• **Málaga** 1881–91/1901   *MEDITERRANEAN SEA*

Above: The Boulevard Montmartre in the early years of the century, when Picasso had just moved to Paris.
Below: Picasso's Le Moulin de la Galette, 1900. In Paris, Picasso rapidly absorbed the lessons of masters like Toulouse-Lautrec. In this painting of the famous café-dancehall in Montmartre Picasso's garish colors make his dancers into sinister creatures of the night.

Early Years in Spain

Pablo Picasso was born in Málaga, southern Spain, in 1881. Even before he could talk, he drew with his fingers in the sand outside his parents' flat. When he learned to speak, it was to ask his mother for pencils.

Picasso's family name was Blasco, a name as common as Smith or Jones. In later life, therefore, Pablo took his mother's family name, Picasso, according to accepted Spanish custom. His father, José Ruiz Blasco, was an artist and teacher. He was a rather dull painter, but with a taste for the unusual and colorful. On one occasion he painted a plaster cast of a head in bright colors: on another he stuck cut-outs of birds to the surface of a picture. Later, Pablo was to take such experiments much further.

Left: Portrait of Doña Maria Picasso Lopez, 1895. Picasso's pastel portrait of his mother shows astonishing mastery in a boy of fourteen.

Above: The city of Málaga, where Picasso was born in 1881. It is a seaport set almost on the southernmost tip of Spain, overlooking the Mediterranean Sea.

Pablo had two younger sisters, but he remained the only son. The whole family, uncles and aunts included, doted on him. From the age of three he was taken to the bullfights. Don José, his father, would explain to him the fine points of the dangerous and bloody ritual contest between man and beast. The bullring was a pageant of costume and color, courage and cruelty, skill and style. Picasso was never to forget it. Throughout his life as an artist in France he remained Spanish to the core. His art would always reflect the vivid contrasts of his native land: dazzling sun and deep shadow, extremes of heat and cold, of wealth and wretched poverty, gaiety and misery, love and cruelty.

In 1891, Don José accepted a post as art master at a school in Corunna, a seaport on the Atlantic coast of northeast Spain. Pablo was ten years old. He began to make such rapid progress in art that he was allowed to work on his father's own

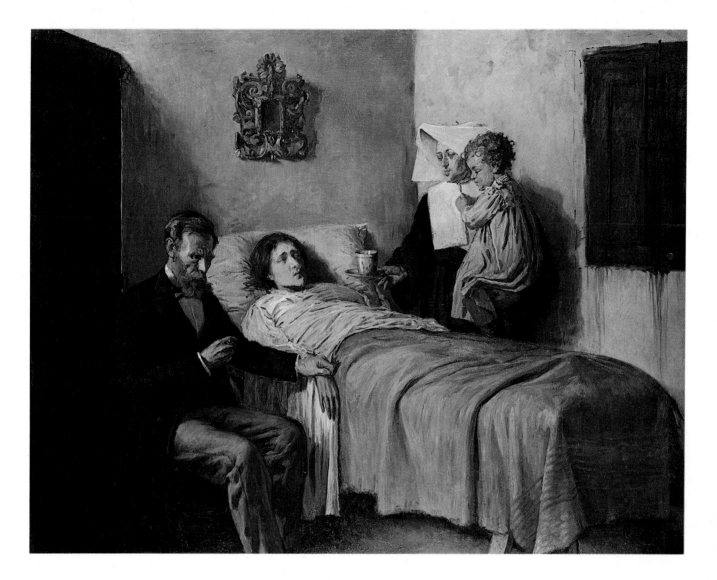

canvases. At last, Don José was so impressed by his son's talent that he handed over his brushes and palette to Pablo, vowing never to paint again.

In 1895, the family moved again, to Barcelona, a bustling Mediterranean port not far south of the French border. Don José joined the staff of the art school; Pablo, barely fourteen, took only a day to sail through entrance exams for which a whole month was normally allowed. Two years later he astonished everybody by repeating the same thing at the Royal Academy in Madrid, the Spanish capital. In the meantime, Pablo completed a large painting, *Science and Charity*, that established his reputation as a young painter of brilliant talent.

In Madrid, Picasso soon found that, technically, he had nothing left to learn. He spent much of his time quietly studying the masterpieces in the Prado, Spain's most famous art museum. He returned to Barcelona in 1899. There he mixed with a group of artists who haunted a tavern called

Above: Science and Charity, *1896. Picasso painted this large picture at the age of sixteen. It is a typically sentimental 19th century subject – much influenced by English painting of the time. In fact, the subject was set as an exercise for Pablo by his father, who also posed for the figure of the doctor.*

Els Quatre Gats ("The Four Cats"). The owner, Père Romeu, had modeled his pub on a cabaret-bar he had known in Paris.

The artists and writers who met at Père Romeu's were proud of their Spanish and Catalan traditions, but they also looked outwards to France and to England. Picasso shared his father's enthusiasm for English art, and in 1900, set out for London. On his way he stopped off in Paris to visit the World Fair. The magic of Paris overwhelmed him and he fell completely under its spell.

Picasso in Paris

During the years 1900 to 1904, Picasso divided his time between Paris and Barcelona, before settling permanently in Paris in 1904. Paris was the greatest center of European art. There he could meet other artists, writers, collectors and dealers. Above all, he could study at first hand the paintings of modern artists like Toulouse-Lautrec, Van Gogh and Munch. Their works had an emotional force that matched his own restless energy. Gradually he absorbed the lessons learned from their pictures into his own developing style. His studio was in a

Below: A modern photograph of the old Lapin Agile, *the Montmartre bar where Picasso and his friends gathered. The circle of Spanish painters and Parisian poets and critics made up* la bande Picasso.

Right: Picasso's Woman in a Chemise, *1905. The finely drawn classical profile of the young woman contrasts with the silvery, ghost-like tones of her body. After 1905, Picasso began to leave his "Blue Period" behind.*

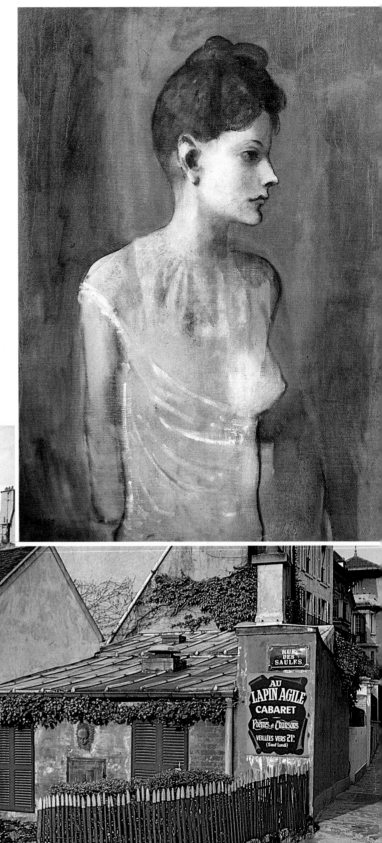

ramshackle apartment block on the hill of Montmartre, overlooking Paris from the north. The block was known as *Le Bateau Lavoir*, because it resembled the laundry boats on the River Seine below.

Picasso's early years in Paris were a time of hardship and poverty. With other struggling young artists, he lived in squalid conditions. The paintings of this time depict lonely, melancholy figures existing, like Picasso himself, outside the borders of society. They are painted in ghostly, unearthly blues, giving rise to the term "Blue Period" for works of the years 1901–1904.

In these years, too, Picasso gradually broke with his family. Once so proud of him, they now disapproved of his shabby appearance and long hair. In Paris, however, serious collectors began to buy his work. He met the American brother and sister Leo and Gertrude Stein. They held regular parties to which they invited a brilliant circle of writers, poets and painters. By 1906, Picasso was probably the best-known young painter in Paris.

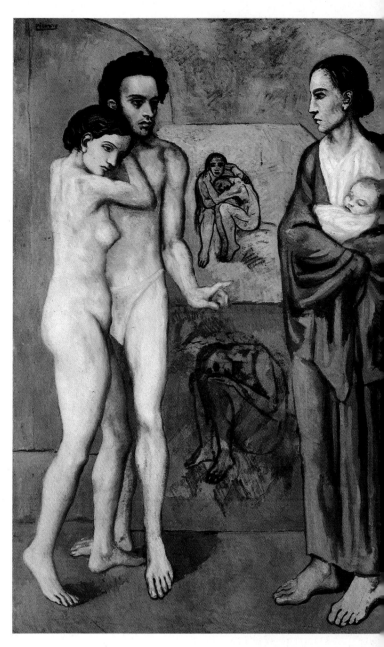

Above: Picasso's La Vie (Life), *1903. This large painting is the most ambitious work of the "Blue Period". It is about love, life and death. The male figure is a likeness of Picasso's close friend Carles Casagenas, who shot himself over the love of a girl in 1901. But the mother and child show that life goes on, despite sadness.*

Left: A photograph of Picasso in 1904, the year he moved permanently to Paris.

13

Montmartre and Montparnasse

Right: Picasso's Portrait of Gertrude Stein, *1906. Gertrude Stein and her brother Leo were American collectors who had settled in Paris about the same time as Picasso.*

When Picasso first arrived in Paris, Montmartre was still a straggling hill village outside Paris. It was dominated by derelict windmills, and by the new, shining white church of Sacre Coeur. Its steep, narrow streets were lined with small houses and old cottages. Scattered patches of wasteland were dotted with the shanties and huts of scrap-dealers and outcasts. It was a perfect refuge for struggling artists and writers. Studios were cheap, and food and drink could be bought for a few cents in the cafés and bistros. Picasso and his friends met in cafés, or visited the dancehalls and nightclubs of the Boulevard Montmartre.

Utrillo's Passage Cottin, Montmartre, *around 1912. Utrillo's romantic views of Montmartre were painted at a time when the old village was already becoming a picturesque tourist attraction. Most of the young artists who had lived there followed Picasso to the Montparnasse district to the south across the Seine.*

In 1912, Picasso and many other artists left Montmartre for Montparnasse, a district on the left bank of the Seine, to the south. Soon the studios and cafés around the Boulevard Montparnasse attracted artists and intellectuals from all over the world. At the heart of the district were the two cafés where everybody met. At the *Café de la Rotonde*, before 1914, Lenin sat plotting revolution. Opposite, the *Café du Dôme* was the haunt of artists like Vlaminck, Modigliani, Derain, Léger, Delaunay and Picasso himself. Until the beginning of World War II, Montparnasse was to be the great center of Modern Art.

Below: In Montparnasse, as in Montmartre, local cafés and bars became the meeting places for the community of painters, writers and poets. The famous Café du Dôme was a favorite haunt of Picasso. It continued its reputation as a center of artistic and intellectual life until World War II.

The Cubist Years

Between 1907 and 1914 Picasso, with his close collaborator Braque, developed an entirely new kind of painting. This movement, Cubism, was the most important step in the history of Modern Art. It was also the greatest change in art for five centuries.

All that time the art of painting had imitated, in one way or another, surface appearances. Objects, beings and the space containing them had been depicted as if seen from a single point of view, rather as one looks through the viewfinder of a camera. But the invention of photography in the 19th century had made this task of painting much less important. Artists were now free to concentrate on truths beyond external appearances.

In Cubist paintings it was no longer possible to recognize objects, figures and spaces at a glance. They had been broken up, flattened out and painstakingly reassembled on the surface of the painting. There was no single point of view but many points of view combined and superimposed. Painters chose to paint what they knew rather than what they saw.

Above: The painter Georges Braque in his studio, 1910.

Left: Picasso's Seated Nude, *1909–1910. In this typical Cubist painting, subject and background are broken up into flat shapes.*

Below: Bottle of Vieux Marc, glass, guitar and newspaper, 1913. This late Cubist work by Picasso is a Papier Collé *(French for "glued paper"). All the objects in the title are to be found in the picture – but the painting has to be "read" to find them.*

FIGARO

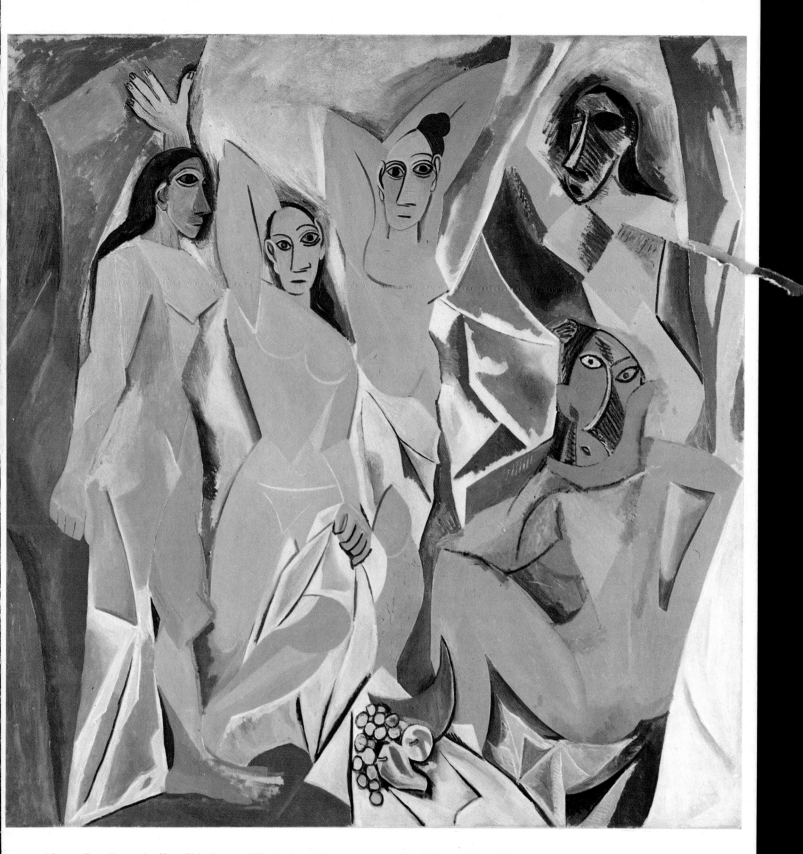

Above: Les Demoiselles d'Avignon. *Early in 1907, visitors to Picasso's studio were astonished by a large and amazingly original canvas on which he was at work. They were disturbed by the violently distorted female nudes and by the grotesque heads, based on African masks, which added to the awesome power of the life-size figures. The three on the left have the clear-cut solidity which Picasso admired in pre-Roman Spanish sculpture. He had already tried out this style in the portrait of Gertrude Stein (p14). The figure in the lower right – twisted and flattened – heralds the Cubist years which followed. Although the painting was never finished, it completely changed the course of 20th century art.*

17

After Cubism

As a result of Cubism, certain artists felt able to produce completely abstract paintings. By abstract they meant paintings which do not represent any object or situation in the real or visible world. Two of the earliest and greatest pioneers of abstraction were Piet Mondrian, from the Netherlands, and Kasimir Malevich, who lived in Moscow. Following Picasso, they both worked their way through Cubism as though learning a new language. But whereas Picasso continued to produce non-Cubist, representational paintings and drawings, Mondrian and Malevich went beyond Cubism. They felt that Cubism had freed them to ignore the world of natural appearances. Each of their paintings would be an object in its own right, with no need to describe other objects. Painters were now free, if they chose, to express ideas and emotions through pure forms and colors rather than through recognisable images.

Picasso and the Ballet

During the war years, Picasso's career took an unexpected direction. In 1917, he was invited to Rome to meet Serge Diaghilev, director of the revolutionary Russian Ballet. Picasso agreed to design the scenery and costumes for a new ballet, *Parade*, by the poet Jean Cocteau. The music was by the Parisian composer Erik Satie. The story was about three rival circus managers, each trying to persuade the public to visit his show. It was given its first performance in Paris in May, 1917 — and nearly caused a riot. The managers' bizarre Cubist costumes towered over three meters high. Satie's "music" was a deafening barrage of weird sounds. The audience was outraged. It took Picasso's friend Apollinaire to restore order. Home on leave with a head wound, dressed in his army uniform, Apollinaire finally managed to convince the audience that *Parade* was not part of some enemy plot. Picasso went on to design several more ballets for Diaghilev. In the meantime, he married one of Diaghilev's dancers Olga Koklova, shown right in a portrait of 1923.

Right: Malevich's Dynamic Suprematism, *1915. A Russian, Malevich was inspired by Cubism to produce abstract pictures like this. He believed that complicated sensations and feelings could be expressed by pure shapes and forms. He invented the term "Suprematism" – meaning "supremacy of feeling".*

Below: Léger's Still Life with a Beermug, *1922. Léger was a Cubist whose work was leading him towards abstraction. But his war service turned him back to a deeper appreciation of people and things in the world. This painting shows his pleasure in simple, modern products – a beermug on a table amid bright patterns.*

Right: Mondrian's Composition with Gray, Red, Yellow and Blue, *1920. Mondrian aimed at universal harmony and balance by restricting himself to the three primary colors, red, yellow and blue, with the tones black, white or gray. These are set in a grid of black lines.*

New Movements in Paris

During the 1920s, the war over, people filtered back to Paris. The community of artists, writers and intellectuals came together again. But there were now new movements and new personalities. Many artists and poets had spent the war years in foreign countries, in neutral centers as far apart as New York, Zurich and Barcelona. In such widely separated places they had managed to keep in touch with each other, using the label *Dada* to describe all their activities. The Dada movement first began in Zurich in 1916. At an arts club called the Cabaret Voltaire, a group of artists and poets put on a bizarre series of entertainments and exhibitions.

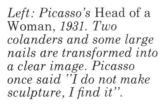

Left: Picasso's Head of a Woman, *1931. Two colanders and some large nails are transformed into a clear image. Picasso once said "I do not make sculpture, I find it".*

Above: The Three Dancers, *1925. Picasso's paintings of the 1920s were very different from the cool, controlled analysis of the Cubist years. They were violent, disturbed, showing the human body almost pulled apart and cruelly distorted. Part of this may have been personal – his marriage with Olga was becoming increasingly unhappy. But the paintings are also influenced by the Surrealists' interest in the dark, savage side of human nature. While Picasso was painting this large picture on a theme of ballet dancers an old friend died – his profile appears in black at top right of the composition. His friend's death affected Picasso deeply, triggering off unhappy memories of their early years in Paris. Urgently, Picasso transformed his picture into a savage dance: at the same time, using Cubist language, he turned the dance into a crucifixion, a universal symbol of death. Today we can see that the greatness of this work lies in the way that Picasso has combined deeply personal feelings with fundamental human experience.*

They proclaimed that they were out to demolish all established standards of good taste. They spouted meaningless gibberish in a deliberate attempt to disgust and outrage their audiences. The name they chose for their performances was *Dada*, French for hobby-horse. The absurd name was the artists' response to the absurd, crazy chaos of the war, which they all regarded as an evil abomination.

From Zurich the spirit of Dada spread to New York, Barcelona, Berlin, Cologne, Hanover and finally Paris. Here the movement changed direction under the leadership of the poet André Breton, who renamed it *Surrealism*. In the spirit of the times, the Surrealists worked for a better, less crazy world. Their aim was to find "the solution of the principal problems of life". Their method was to explore the repressed savagery and irrationalism of the human personality. They attached the greatest importance to the *unconscious* workings of the mind – to dreams, jokes, games, random thoughts and fantasies.

All the Surrealists, painters and poets alike, were inspired by Pablo Picasso. They were well aware of his development of Cubism: and they were particularly excited by the barbaric, primitive energies of his large 1907 painting *Les Demoiselles d'Avignon*. Although Picasso was not a true Surrealist he liked their company. Contact with them triggered off a new phase of his painting, one of remarkable strength, energy and originality – all of which we can see in *The Three Dancers*.

Above: Nude Woman in a Red Armchair, *1932. In stark contrast to* The Three Dancers *opposite, Picasso is able to make distortion express warmth and tenderness.*

The Surrealists

Surrealism deeply affected the arts of painting, sculpture, literature, theater and the cinema during the 20s and 30s. The method was to shock people out of normal methods of thought into strange and imaginative new connections. Painters like Salvador Dali and Magritte showed common objects in unexpected surroundings, dramatically altering their scale and textures. Dali painted pocket watches that seemed to be made of some soft, jelly-like substance. Magritte gave loaves of bread the texture and solidity of ancient stone sculpture. Max Ernst created monsters and dreamscapes. Other artists, like Miro, created abstract paintings in a trance-like state as a way of bypassing normal rational control. The film maker Luis Bunuel created weird, horrific images in films like *Le Chien Andalou* (1928) and *L'Age d'Or* (1930).

Right: A still from the Surrealist film Le Chien Andalou.

Images of War

The 1930s in Europe saw the rise of military dictatorships and wholesale political terror. In 1936, the fascist forces led by General Franco rebelled against the Republican government of Spain. Picasso spoke out against Franco and "the military caste which has sunk Spain in an ocean of pain and death". As the Spanish Civil War continued, Nazi Germany, under Adolf Hitler, backed Franco's rebellion.

In April 1937 the world was horrified when Nazi bombers destroyed the peaceful Basque town of Guernica. Under Franco's orders, German pilots machine-gunned the screaming citizens as they fled. In Paris, Picasso could do far more than issue public statements condemning the atrocity. At 55, he was at the height of his powers and already the most famous living artist. In under two months he produced the greatest canvas of his life and very probably of the entire 20th century – *Guernica*. This epic painting was born out of a particular event. But its tragic anguish grieves for the innocent victims of all wars. Later, Picasso wrote: "No, painting is not done to decorate apartments. It is an instrument for attack and defence against the enemy".

Above: There are no colors in Guernica. *Blacks, whites, grays, sombre tones and harsh contrasts were more fitting for Picasso's tragic theme. The whole picture sums up and combines all that Picasso had learned in all the brilliant phases of his art. The intense emotionalism of his "Blue Period" is expressed here in dramatic gestures. They are combined with the fragmentation of shape and the flattened space of Cubism. The sinister, distorted forms of* The Three Dancers *are used here to convey chaotic violence. The imagery is Spanish. The horse, innocent casualty in so many bullfights, rears up with a spear through the belly in an effort to avoid the prostrate form of a man whose severed hand still grips a broken sword. The massive head of the bull – at once victim and aggressor – watches over the grief-racked figure of a mother whose dead baby lies in her arms. Elsewhere, women rush to avoid the searing flames. All the while a naked light bulb, whose rays are jagged teeth, surveys the whole tragic scene like an unblinking evil eye.* Guernica *is Picasso's great public statement on the horrors of war. But after its rapid completion, Picasso continued to pour out his emotion in much smaller, private works.*

Left: Weeping Woman, *1937. This painting is the last and strongest of a series on the same theme. Its discordant combination of acid colors, its jagged shapes and distortions transmit an overwhelming concentration of bitterness and convey the shattering effect of violence on humanity.*

Year	Picasso's Life	Other Events
1917	In Rome designs costumes and sets for Russian Ballet Company; Meets Olga Koklova, one of the dancers; May 18, Paris, first performance of ballet *Parade* on which Picasso has worked with Cocteau and Eric Satie.	October Revolution in Russia; Lenin appointed chief Commissar.
1918	Picasso and Olga married; They move to apartment in expensive district near the Champs-Elysées.	Armistice signed between Allies and Germany ends World War I.
1921	Picasso's first son, Paolo, born.	Death of Eric Satie, French composer.
1925	Picasso represented in first Surrealist exhibition with Arp, Ernst, Klee, Miro and others; Paints *The Three Dancers*.	Chrysler Corporation founded; Hitler published Volume I of *Mein Kampf*.
1928	Starts to make sculpture again after 14 year break.	First Mickey Mouse animated cartoon, *Steamboat Willie, Junior*.
1929	Learns technique of welding from Spanish sculptor Julio Gonzalez.	Diaghilev dies in Venice; Salvador Dali joins the Surrealists in Paris; First sound film, *The Jazz Singer*.
1934	Extended visit to Spain: Madrid, San Sebastian, Toledo; Paints many bullfight scenes; Separates from Olga.	Hitler and Mussolini meet in Venice.
1935	Picasso's daughter Maria born to Marie-Thérèse Walter.	Nazi government in Germany introduce compulsory military service.
1936	Summer in south of France with Dora Maar; The Spanish Republican government appoint Picasso director of the Prado Museum in Madrid.	Spanish Civil War begins in July; General Franco appointed Chief of State by rebels in October.
1937	Dora Maar photographs Guernica in several successive stages of completion before it is exhibited in Spanish Pavilion at Paris World Fair.	First jet engine built by Frank Whittle in Britain; Neville Chamberlain Prime Minister of Britain, begins policy of appeasement; Spanish rebels take Málaga, Picasso's birthplace, and order the destruction of Guernica by German bombers.
1939	Major exhibition of Picasso's work at Museum of Modern Art, New York; Death of his mother.	Germany invades Poland; Britain and France declare war on Germany, September 3.
1940	Remains in Paris despite German occupation; Nazis forbid him to exhibit.	London *Blitz*; Pearl Harbor.
1943	Produces *Bull's Head* and other sculptures using ready-made materials.	Jackson Pollock's first one-man show in New York; Henry Moore's *Madonna and Child*, Northampton.
1944	Joins Communist Party.	Allies make D-Day landings in Normandy; Paris liberated August 25; First atomic bomb dropped on Hiroshima, Japan.
1946	Most of the year spent on French Riviera with Françoise Gilot.	Nazi leaders sentenced to death at Nuremberg.
1947	Picasso's son Claude born to Françoise.	Scientists invent the transistor; Heyerdahl sails on a balsa-wood raft from Peru to Polynesia.
1949	Picasso's daughter Paloma born.	USSR tests its first atom bomb.
1953	Exhibitions in Rome, Milan, Lyon and Sao Paolo; Separates from Françoise.	Stalin dies.
1955	With Jacqueline Roque, Picasso moves into *La Californie*, a villa above Cannes.	Italy, West Germany and France establish European Union; West Germany joins NATO.
1958	Picasso buys the Château de Vauvenargues near Aix-en-Provence.	US nuclear submarine *Nautilus* passes under North Polar ice-cap; European Common Market established.
1961	Moves to large villa, Notre-Dame-de-Vie at Mougins, near Cannes.	J F Kennedy 35th President of the USA, meets Khrushchev in Vienna for disarmament talks.
1963	Picasso Museum founded in Barcelona.	President Kennedy assassinated; Lee Harvey Oswald, presumed assassin, shot and killed by Jack Ruby.
1965	Designs iron sculpture over 20 meters high for Chicago's new Civic Center.	Unilateral Declaration of Independence by Rhodesia; US astronaut walks outside spaceship for 21 minutes.
1967	Exhibitions of Picasso's sculpture at Tate Gallery, London and the Museum of Modern Art, New York.	Six Day War between Israel and Arab nations led by Egypt.
1971	Exhibitions in Paris celebrate Picasso's 90th birthday.	Women granted the vote in Switzerland; Cigarette advertisements banned from US television.
1973	Picasso dies at Mougins, April 8.	Energy crisis; Arab oil embargo forces cutbacks in America, Western Europe and Japan; Great Britain, Denmark and Ireland join the European Common Market.

Picasso's Greatest Works

Paintings: *Le Moulin de la Galette* 1900 (90 × 116 cm) Solomon R. Guggenheim Museum, New York.

La Vie 1903 (197 × 127·3 cm) Museum of Art, Cleveland.

Family of Saltimbanques (acrobats) 1905 (212·8 × 229·6 cm) National Gallery, Washington.

Portrait of Gertrude Stein 1906 (100 × 81 cm) Metropolitan Museum of Art, New York.

Les Demoiselles d'Avignon 1907 (244 × 233 cm) Museum of Modern Art, New York.

Portrait of Ambroise Vollard 1910 (93 × 66 cm) Pushkin Museum, Moscow.

Still-Life with Chair-caning 1912 (29 × 37 cm) Artist's estate. (This is the first collage.)

Bottle, Glass and Violin (papier collé) 1913 (47 × 62·5 cm) Moderna Museet, Stockholm.

The Three Musicians 1921 (203 × 188 cm) Museum of Art, Philadelphia.

Seated Woman 1923 (92 × 73 cm) Tate Gallery, London.

The Three Dancers 1925 (215 × 142 cm) Tate Gallery, London.

Guernica 1937 (350·5 × 782·3 cm) Museum of Modern Art, New York. (On extended loan from the artist's estate.)

Weeping Woman 1937 (60 × 49 cm) Tate Gallery, London (lent anonymously).

Night Fishing at Antibes 1939 (202·9 × 350·2 cm) Museum of Modern Art, New York.

Las Meninas 1957 (194 × 260 cm) Museo Picasso, Barcelona.

Sculpture: *Head of a Woman (Fernande)* 1909 bronze (height 42 cm) Museum of Modern Art, New York.

Glass of Absinthe 1914 painted bronze (height 22 cm) Museum of Art, Philadelphia.

Still Life 1914 painted wood with upholstery fringe (25·5 × 48 × 10 cm) Tate Gallery, London.

Construction in Wire 1928 (50 × 41 × 17 cm) Artist's estate.

Bull's Head 1943 bronze (42 × 41 × 15 cm) Artist's estate.

Man with a Lamb 1944 bronze (22 × 78 × 72 cm) Presented by Picasso in 1950 to the town of Vallauris, France, where it now stands in the central square.

Glossary

Collage Painting made up of pieces of cloth, paper or other materials stuck to the picture surface. The technique was invented by Picasso in 1912; its name derives from the French *coller* – "to stick".

Cubism Name given to the movement which grew out of the efforts of Picasso and Braque to create paintings not based on surface appearances. They superimposed different viewpoints and painted what they understood about a subject rather than what could be seen at a particular time. Subject and background are flattened onto the picture surface by dividing it into fragments and planes. Originally developed between 1907 and 1908, Cubism paved the way for abstract painting.

Dada Nonsense word invented to describe an art movement which set out to ridicule and outrage ordinary society. It began during World War I, to merge into Surrealism in the next decade in Paris.

Fauvism School of painting in Paris led by Matisse, Derain and Vlaminck. The boldness and violence of their paintings led a critic to call them *"Les Fauves"*, meaning "wild beasts".

Objet Trouvé ("found object") Any ready-made object transformed by the artist by including it in a work of art. From 1914 Picasso began to include such objects as spoons, nails, colanders in his sculptures. The method was adopted by many Surrealists, who like Picasso attached great significance to the *finding* of an object and setting it in an unexpected context.

Surrealism Term coined by Apollinaire to describe truths and realities beyond visible appearances. During the 20s and 30s in Paris Surrealist artists and writers experimented with ways of revealing and expressing a hidden world of imagination, dreams and unconscious desires.

Galleries to Visit

List of major galleries showing works by Picasso:
France: Musée National d'Art Moderne (Centre Pompidou), Paris; Musée d'Art Moderne de la Ville de Paris.
Germany: Kunstsammlung Nordrhein-Westfalen, Dusseldorf.
Great Britain: The Tate Gallery, London.
Netherlands: Stedelijk Museum, Amsterdam; Gemeente Museum, the Hague; Rijksmuseum Kröller-Müller, Otterlo.
Norway: National Gallery, Oslo.
Spain: Picasso Museum, Barcelona.
Sweden: National Museum, Stockholm.
Switzerland: Kunstmuseum, Basle.
USA: Museum of Modern Art, New York; Metropolitan Museum of Art, New York; Solomon R. Guggenheim Museum, New York; Museum of Fine Arts, Boston; Museum of Art, Cleveland; Museum of Art, Philadelphia; Art Institute, Chicago; National Gallery, Washington.
USSR: Pushkin Museum, Moscow; Museum of Modern Western Art, Moscow; Hermitage Museum, Leningrad.

Books to Read

Pablo Picasso by Miranda Smith (Creative Education) — written for young people
Picasso: his life and work by Roland Penrose (Harper and Row) — the standard biography full of essential information
Picasso: Fifty Years of his Art by Alfred H. Barr Jr. (Museum of Modern Art, New York) — the great classic on Picasso's art
The World of Picasso by Lael Wertenbaker (Time-Life) — a selection from the Library of Art

Acknowledgements

Picture Research: Penny Warn and Tracy Rawlings
All the works by Pablo Picasso which appear in this book and the work by M. Utrillo on page 15, F. Léger on page 19 and P. Mondrian on page 19 are © S.P.A.D.E.M. Paris, 1980.
Photographs: Camera Press 4–5; Collection of the Art Institute of Chicago/For the Civic Center Chicago 25 bottom left; The Cleveland Museum of Art, Gift of the Hanna Fund 1945 13 top; Contemporary Films Ltd 21 bottom; Collection of Mr. and Mrs. Victor W. Ganz 23 bottom right; Document, Claude Laurens 16 top; Metropolitan Museum of Art, Bequest of G. Stein 1946 14; The Museum of Modern Art New York, 22–23, 17 (Lillie P. Bliss Bequest); The Picasso Museum, Barcelona 10 bottom, 11, 24 bottom left; Picturepoint 10 top; Popperfoto 6 bottom, 23 bottom left; The Prado Museum, Madrid 24 bottom right; Private Collection 6; Private Collection London 22; Radio Times Hulton Picture Library 9 top; Scala/Thannhauser Collection, New York 9 bottom; Snark International 8 bottom; Tate Gallery 15, 16, 19, 20 top, 21 top; The Daily Telegraph Colour Library 12; Verlag Gerd Hatje/John Hedgecoe 7 25 center, /Chevojon, Paris 20 bottom, 25 bottom right, /Brassai, Paris 25 top; National Gallery of Art. Washington/Chester Dale Collection 18;
Cover Spectrum; Popperfoto; Endpapers The Museum of Modern Art, New York/Mrs. Simon Guggenheim Fund.

Index